Cells, Tissues and Organs

Donna Latham

Chicago, Illinois

Customer Service 888-454-2279
Visit our website at www.heinemannraintree.com

Editorial: Megan Cotugno and Andrew Farrow
Design: Philippa Jenkins
Illustrations: KJA-artists.com
Picture Research: Ruth Blair
Production: Alison Parsons
Originated by Modern Age
Printed and bound in China by CTPS

15 14
10 9 8 7 6 5

Library of Congress Cataloging-in-Publication Data
Latham, Donna.
  Cells, tissues, and organs / Donna Latham.
     p. cm. -- (Sci-hi: life science)
  Includes bibliographical references and index.
  ISBN 978-1-4109-3239-6 (hc) -- ISBN 978-1-4109-3254-9 (pb) 1. Human biology--Popular works. I. Title.
  QP34.5.L39 2008
  612--dc22
                          2008026149

Acknowledgments
The author and publishers are grateful to the following for permission to reproduce copyright material: © Corbis/Cloud Hill Imaging Ltd p. **20**; © Corbis/Duomo p. **6**; © Corbis/Jack Hollingsworth p. **28**; © Corbis/Goodshoot p. **30**; © Corbis/MedicalRF.com p. **35**; © Corbis/Micha Pawlitzki/Zefa p. **26**; © Corbis/Micro Discovery p. **5**; © Corbis/NASA p. **4**; © Corbis/Visuals Unlimited p. **7**; © Photoshot p. **25**; Photoshot/UPPA pp. **9**, **10**; © Science Photo Library pp. **iii** (Contents, bottom), **8**, **13**; © Science Photo Library/Adrian T. Sumner p. **16**; © Science Photo Library/Colin Cuthbert p. **41**; © Science Photo Library/Dr. Jeremy Burgess p. **12**; © Science Photo Library/Edward Kinsman pp. **iii** (Contents, top), **23**; © Science Photo Library/Eye of Science p. **15**; © Science Photo Library/Martin Shields p. **17**; © Science Photo Library/Omikron p. **12**; © Science Photo Library/Scott Bauer/U.S. Dept. of Agriculture p. **14**; © Science Photo Library/ Sovereign, ISM p. **32**; © Science Photo Library/Steve Gschmeissner pp. **22**, **25**, **27**, **40**; © Shutterstock background images and design features throughout.

Cover photographs reproduced with permission of © Science Photo Library/Eye of Science **main**; © Science Photo Library/Centre Jean Perrin **inset**.

The publishers would like to thank literacy consultants Nancy Harris, Patti Suerth, and Monica Szalaj, and content consultant Dr. Michelle Raabe for their assistance in the preparation of this book.

Every effort has been made to contact copyright holders of any material reproduced in this book. Any omissions will be rectified in subsequent printings if notice is given to the publisher.

Some words are shown in bold, **like this**. These words are explained in the glossary. You will find important information and definitions underlined and in bold, **like this**.

Contents

Why do cuts and scrapes itch as they heal?

Go to page 23 for the answer!

What is this cell that helps keep you alive?

Go to page 8 to find out!

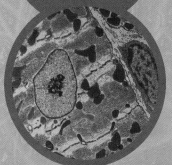

Cells

Cells are the smallest units of life. Cells are called life's building blocks. All living things are formed of cells.

Life's Building Blocks

Visualize any type of small insect. Now imagine an energetic animal and a green plant. You might picture a tarantula, a sea otter, and poison ivy. What on Earth do you share with this odd trio? You all inhabit the same planet. You are all living things.

<u>**Every living thing on this planet is made of cells.**</u>
That includes the human body. Most cells are too tiny to see with the naked eye. To view cells, you must use a microscope, which magnifies them. When you view microscopic cells, you'll discover even smaller parts within them. Just *how* tiny are cells? Visualize the pointy tip of a pin. One million red blood cells could fit on the tip!

Some living things are only made of one cell. For example, **bacteria** are single-celled microorganisms. They survive independently, without other cells. Other living things are made of millions and millions of cells. They have specialized cells that work as a team. Your body is made up of around 10 trillion cells. Suppose you tried to count them? It would take 2,600 years!

All living things on planet Earth are made of the smallest units of life. What are these smallest units of life?

What Do All Cells Have in Common?

- Cells use energy.
- Cells are made of moving parts.
- Cells grow.
- Cells repair damage done to them.
- Cells divide, or split.
- Cells die.

All living things are made up of cells. Below is a magnified image of red blood cells.

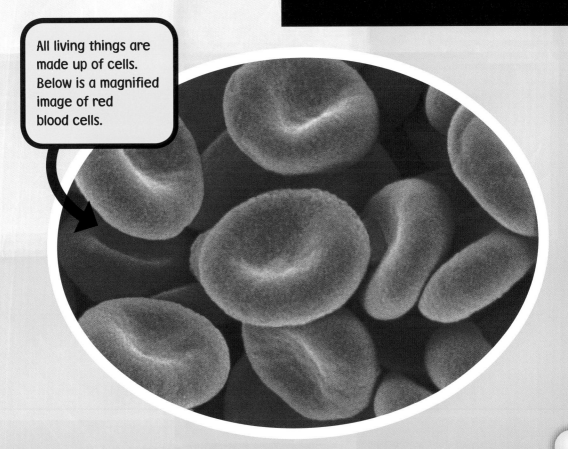

Staying Alive

Like you, cells are alive. Like all living things, cells die at some point. Until that time, cells do what is necessary for survival.

Cells have a lot of work to do. They need energy to tackle their jobs. Most cells get energy through **respiration**, as they combine oxygen and food. They use materials in food to repair injuries and to grow. They clear out wastes and reproduce.

Teamwork

On a basketball court, all the players sizzle on high alert. One player responds when an opposing player closes in. How? She fakes a pass to a teammate. Luckily, the opponent falls for the trick.

Like all successful teams, many cells and bacteria can communicate. For example, cells perform jobs with other cells. Working together, they sense changes in their environment. They react to them. A sports team huddles and works together to achieve a common goal. In the same way, cells group together to get jobs done, as they do in this photo of the human intestines (right).

Cells often group and work together, like these players.

These human intestinal cells work together, like players on a team, to get the job done.

Celebrate Cells

The longest cells in the human body are motor neurons. They can stretch as long as 1.7 meters, or 4.5 feet. Speaking of feet, motor neurons run from the bottom of the spine to the big toe.

How long does it take a single red blood cell to run the entire course of your body? Less than 60 seconds! During that same time, up to 200 million other cells die in the body.

Review

Why are cells called life's building blocks? All living things are made of cells. How many cells are in the human body? There are trillions. What do all cells have in common? They use energy and have moving parts. They repair damage done to them, divide, and die. How do cells work as a team? They communicate and respond to changes.

Levels of Organization

Living things are organized to work cooperatively. **Cells, tissues, organs, and systems form levels. Starting with cells, each level builds upon the other.**

A **hierarchy** is something broken into levels. A hierarchy shows how something is organized. Plants and animals are made of parts that do special jobs. You can break their parts into levels. These levels are cells, tissues, organs, and organ systems.

One Into Another

It all starts with cells, those tiny building blocks. Here's how. Cells are organized into tissues, tissues into organs. Organs are organized into organ systems.

Cells → Tissues → Organs → Organ Systems

Complicated systems all begin with and build from the cell. Through amazing teamwork, like players in a sport, cells, tissues, and organs work together.

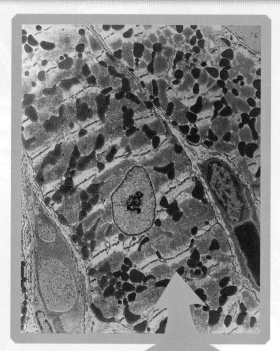

This is a magnified image of a human heart muscle cell.

Life Processes

Biology is the study of life. Biologists identify seven life processes that organisms carry out. These life processes are common to all living things, which, as you've learned, are made of cells.

- **M**ovement—being able to move
- **R**espiration—receiving energy from food
- **S**ensitivity—responding to stimuli or changes
- **G**rowth—becoming larger
- **R**eproduction—making more of itself
- **E**xcretion—passing out wastes
- **N**utrition—taking in food

Need a shortcut to remember an organism's life processes? <u>**MRS. GREN**</u> is glad to help.

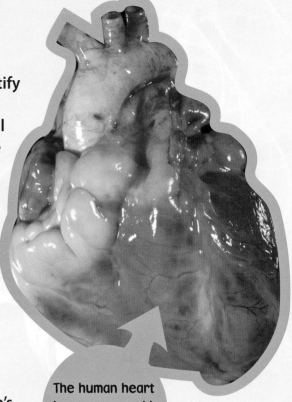

The human heart is an organ and is made of muscle.

Activity

LEVEL IT

Create a visual that shows the levels of organization. Include cells, tissues, organs, and organ systems.

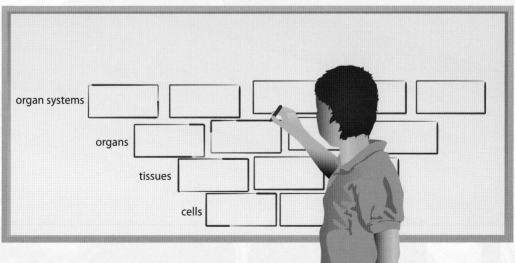

Teamwork

Success depends upon teamwork, just as the body depends upon its systems to function.

Like players on the basketball court, body systems work together. These complicated systems all begin with the cell.

On the Court and In the Body

The clock is running. The score is tied. The crowd wildly screams. In the heat of the game, the players work as hard as they can. What's helping them? The human body's amazing **hierarchy** of cells, tissues, organs, and systems. Bodies are doing their jobs. So the basketball teams can, too.

A player thunders down the court. He's totally focused on the game. He never realizes his musculoskeletal system, formed of muscles and the skeleton, is at work. His legs, large bones and muscles made of tissues, provide movement. Smaller bones and muscles, in the arms and shoulders, help him dribble and shoot. The player's skull protects his brain from injury. His eyes, organs of sight, sweep across the court. They watch for opponents and keep teammates in sight.

Cool!

The game heats up. So does the player. Inside his body's control tower— the brain—the **hypothalamus** checks his temperature. This cooling center sends a message along nerves. The message reaches sweat glands, which get to work. The player perspires. Little droplets cool his skin. Refreshed, he leaps for the net.

Muscles and Bones

▶ Move your legs, arms, and shoulders. How do muscles and bones work together in the actions?

▶ Now, flex your arm muscles. Feel the way they are connected to bone.

Early Investigations, Early Microscopes

How do we know about **cells?** Two famous scientists used microscopes to take a close look at living things. Their investigations paved the way in learning about cells.

Cells → Tissues → Organs → Organ Systems

It is the year 1665. You are in a room in London, hunched over the microscope you created. You peer at thin slices of cork, made from an oak tree. The surface is full of pores, or tiny little holes. It reminds you of a piece of honeycomb.

"These pores, or cells, are the first ever seen," you declare. You are right. You have just discovered plant cells. In fact, you are the first person to use the word *cells*. Who are you? **Robert Hooke**, an English scientist.

Robert Hooke's drawing of cork cells

Drawing of Hooke's microscope

It is the year 1674. A very curious person, you've built many microscopes. During a trip to London, you once viewed Hooke's drawings. They impressed you and influenced you to do your own research.

Now, you collect greenish water samples from a lake in Delft, Holland. You study them under your microscope. They are wiggling! It's an entire living world you have never observed before. These moving things, you decide, are tiny animals. What will you call them? *Animalcules.*

In 1683 you scrape tartar samples from your own teeth. You view them with your microscope. They are wiggling, too. You don't realize it, but the moving objects you've discovered are **protozoa** and **bacteria**. They are single-celled microorganisms. Who are you? **Antoni van Leeuwenhoek**, a Dutch lens maker and scientist.

Antoni van Leeuwenhoek's drawing of his microscope.

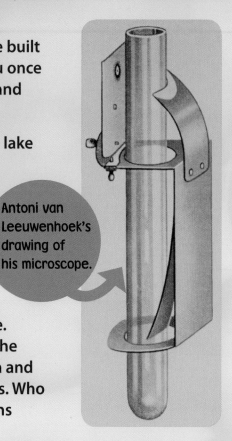

REVIEW

Who? *Robert Hooke (1635–1703)*

When? *1665*

What? *Discovered plant cells*

Where? *London, England*

How? *Studied cork*

Who? *Antoni van Leeuwenhoek (1632–1723)*

When? *1674, 1683*

What? *Discovered protozoa and bacteria*

Where? *Delft, Holland*

How? *Studied water samples and teeth scrapings*

Inside Cells

Today, scientists use electron microscopy to study tiny **cells**. Cells are made of little parts called **organelles**. Animal and plant cells are different in structure.

Today's electron microscopes are very high tech.

Hooke's and van Leeuwenhoek's microscopic discoveries were important stepping stones. With advances in technology, microscopes are far more complex. Today, scientists use electron microscopy. Electron microscopes magnify cells two million times.

To view cells, scientists stain them with dye. Colors include red, blue, and violet. Dyes help different parts of cells pop out. Then, scientists easily view them. And what shapes they observe! Some cells look like flowers, rods, or chunks of coral. Others appear to be weird blobs, or like UFOs or sea creatures. Healthy red blood cells resemble puffy doughnuts. Those that show sickle cell anemia are crescent shaped. They resemble miniature sickles, or curved blades.

Inside one drop of blood are millions of tiny red blood cells. Imagine the number in the 4.7 liters (10 pints) of blood flowing through the average human body! Study the photos of these different blood cells. How would you describe them?

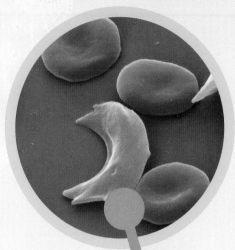

Healthy red blood cells and a sickle cell (left)

Compare and contrast

A Venn diagram uses overlapping circles to compare and contrast two things. The sides include features that are different. The overlapping area shows features that are the same. Make a Venn diagram. Compare and contrast views of the blood cells in the photos.

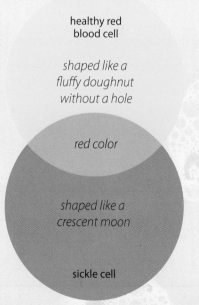

healthy red blood cell

shaped like a fluffy doughnut without a hole

red color

shaped like a crescent moon

sickle cell

Parts of Cells

Cells are extremely tiny. It might be hard to imagine they're made of even smaller movable parts. These parts are called **organelles**, which means "little organs." Each organelle has a special function, or job that is perfect for it.

Inside the Nucleus

Did you know plant and animal cells couldn't survive without a **nucleus**? It's true! The nucleus is the largest, most important part of the cell. It's like the cell's brain. Inside the nucleus are rod-shaped **chromosomes**. Made of the chemical DNA, chromosomes give living things their characteristics. They are important messengers. Chromosomes carry instructions that tell each cell to do its job. Chromosomes also hold **genes**. Genes pass information from one generation to the next. Is your hair curly or straight? What color are your eyes? Do you have freckles? Genes that determine those traits have been passed along from your parents.

This is a magnified human chromosome.

Cheeky!

- Before you begin, make certain you completely scrub your hands with soap and water.

- SOFTLY scrape the inside of your cheek. Use the wider end of a clean, flat-edged toothpick.

- Next, mount the scraping on a clean, dry slide. Add one drop of stain. Place a slipcover over the drop and let it set for 60 seconds.

- Then, observe your cheek cells under a microscope. Illustrate what you see. Save your illustration for the next activity!

You can easily collect cells by carefully scraping the inside of your cheek.

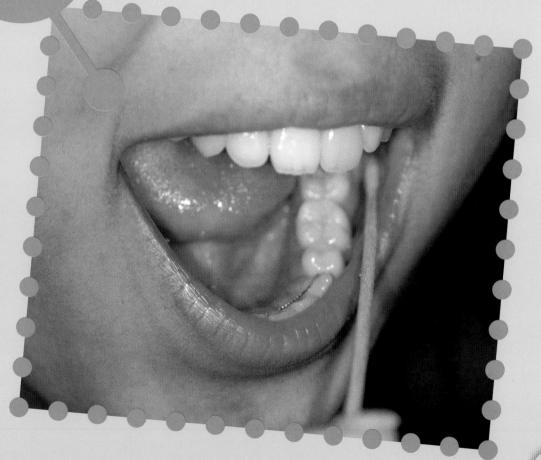

Basic Animal Cell

Take a close look at organelles and their functions in a basic animal cell. Study the diagram. Read the chart to learn about shapes and appearances. Find out what special job each organelle is in charge of.

This is a diagram of a basic animal cell, with the organelles labeled.

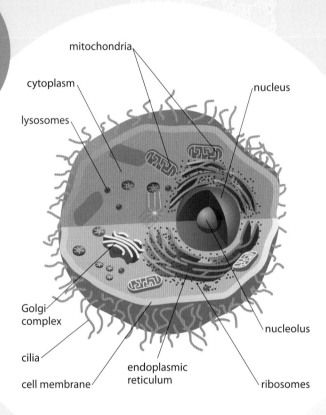

mitochondria

cytoplasm

nucleus

lysosomes

Golgi complex

cilia

cell membrane

endoplasmic reticulum

nucleolus

ribosomes

Cheeky again!

You've learned more about cell parts. Now, label the cell membrane, cytoplasm, and nucleus on your cheek cell illustration.

Basic Animal Cell

Organelle	Shape/Appearance	Function/Job Description
Nucleus	Big and round	The nucleus is the cell's brain. It controls the cell.
Nucleolus	Little round body	The nucleolus is inside the nucleus. It puts together ribosomes, which are bunches of protein.
Cell Membrane	Like separate pieces of plastic wrap	The cell membrane holds the cell together.
Cilia	Hair-like threads	Cilia move fluids over the cell.
Cytoplasm	Rubbery fluid	Cytoplasm is everything in a cell except the nucleus. It contains tiny structures.
Endoplasmic Reticulum (ER)	Network of tubes and sacs; some endoplasmic reticulum surfaces are smooth; others have ribosomes on them and are rough	Smooth endoplasmic reticulum makes carbohydrates (sugars) and lipids (fats). Rough endoplasmic reticulum makes proteins.
Golgi Complex	A pile of flat sacs	The Golgi complex modifies and moves carbohydrates, lipids, and proteins from the endoplasmic reticulum.
Lysosomes	Little and round	Lysosomes handle digestion. They contain enzymes that break down and recycle substances to aid digestion.
Mitochondria	Oblong	Mitochondria change food into energy. They are the cell's powerhouses.
Ribosomes	Little and round	Ribosomes make proteins.

Basic Plant Cell

Unlike other living things, plants make their own food. This process is called **photosynthesis**. Because of this incredible ability, plant cells are different from animal cells. Plant cells have a few more structures.

What's the major difference between animal and plant cells? It's the presence of orgenelles called **chloroplasts**. Photosynthesis takes place in chloroplasts. Chloroplasts are mini solar panels! Inside them is **chlorophyll**, a green pigment. Chlorophyll gives plants their green color. It snatches solar energy and helps chloroplasts do their job.

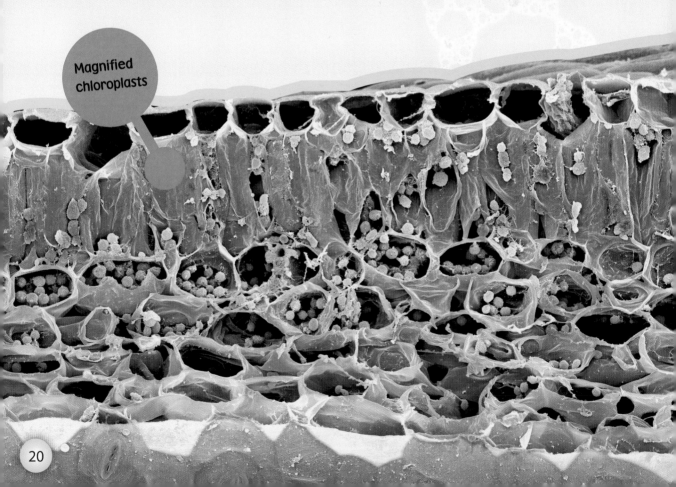

Magnified chloroplasts

The chart below shows plant organelles and their functions.

ADDITIONAL ORGANELLES IN PLANT CELLS

Organelle	Shape/Appearance	Function/Job Description
Cell Wall	Made of stiff but stretchy cellulose	The cell wall is the outside layer of the cell. It stretches as the cell grows. The cell wall protects the cell and holds its shape.
Chloroplast	Rod-shaped sac	It is full of a fluid called chlorophyll. This is where photosynthesis takes place.
Vacuole	Bag filled with fluid	Found in the cytoplasm of the cell, the vacuole holds pigments, or substances that give color; water; and waste products.

A 3-D Model

Choose an animal cell or a plant cell. Then, create a 3-D model of the cell and label its parts. Be creative in your choice of materials! You might use clay or gelatin. You could even bake a sheet cake. Add different-colored frostings to show organelles. Or use bits and pieces like cotton balls, pasta, rice, and ribbon.

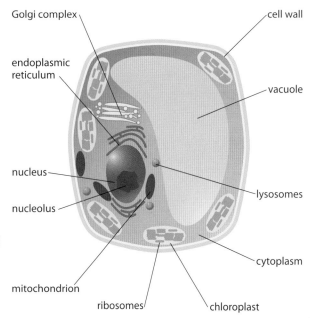

Cells to the Rescue

When a wound develops, the body seems to magically heal itself. In fact, cells are just doing their jobs.

You're having a great time skateboarding. Unfortunately, you don't see the crack in the curb. In the blink of an eye, you tumble forward and land hard on your elbow. Blood trickles from a cut. That means tiny blood vessels under the epidermis have torn. At home, you clean the wound. Luckily, it is not serious. You squeeze on antibacterial ointment and bandage it.
Now what?

Your body, like an emergency medical team, springs into action. **Platelets**, which are saucer-shaped pieces of cells in the blood, respond. They clump together to clot, or thicken, around torn blood vessels. Soon, the bleeding stops.

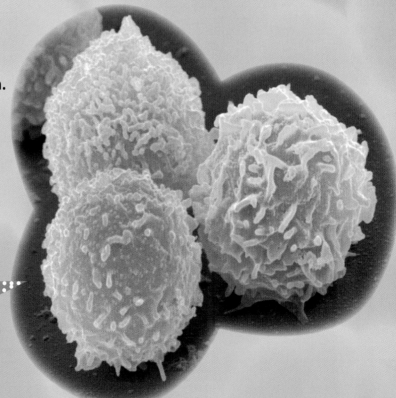

Magnified white blood cells

In several days, a lumpy scab develops. This crusty covering is actually a dried blood clot. It protects the wound like a helmet and allows your body to heal itself. The skin around the scab reddens. It feels hot to the touch. What's happening under this scab?

Cells to the rescue! First, white blood cells attack the wound. They gobble germs that crept inside torn skin. Next, **fibroblasts**—large, flat cells—make **collagen**. They fill the wound with oxygen-rich blood. New blood vessels sprout.

Then, epithelial cells circle the wound. They clump together to make new cells. Fibroblasts pitch in again. They tug the sides of the wound, closing them.

After about two weeks, the scab falls off. New skin covers that area on your elbow.

Many cellular processes are taking place as this wound is healing.

DID YOU KNOW?

Wounds itch as they heal. It's because of nerve fibers that grow inflamed in response to pain. Why? Healing wounds shrink and tug on the scab, causing pain. Ouch!

Review

What role do white blood cells play in healing wounds? They attack germs that enter into broken skin. **How do epithelial cells help?** They circle the wound and make new cells.

Tissues

Cells of the same type that perform the same job group together. They form tissues, the second level of the hierarchy. There are four types of tissues in the human body. Plants have three different types of tissues.

Cells → Tissues → Organs → Organ Systems

You know cells are life's building blocks. Imagine those blocks stacking. Cells work with cells of the same type to form tissues. Tissues perform special functions.

Body Tissues

In the human body, there are four major types of tissues. They are connective, epithelial, muscle, and nerve tissues.

Connective tissues connect and support body parts and organs. They work as padding under your skin. Bone and cartilage are connective tissues. So are inner layers of skin and tendons. Even blood is a connective tissue.

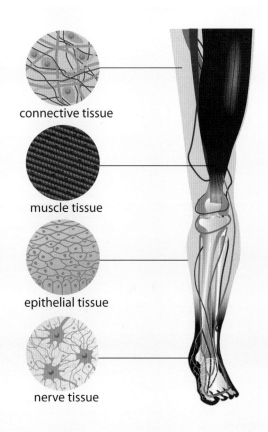

connective tissue

muscle tissue

epithelial tissue

nerve tissue

Epithelial tissues are firmly bunched together. They create protective layers that line various areas of the body. They also surround organs. Run your fingertips over your arm. You've just touched epithelial tissue. It's in the outer layer of skin. Epithelial tissue also lines the inside of your mouth.

Muscle tissues can contract, or tighten up, and relax. Muscle tissues make your heart beat. They pump fluids throughout the body. They also move body parts. One example is the contracting tissue of the biceps. This large muscle in your upper arm contracts when you move your elbow. Another is the deltoid. This triangle-shaped muscle covers the joint at the front of your shoulder.

Nerve tissues transmit electrical signals. Messages move from the brain down the spinal cord. They travel to other areas of the body.

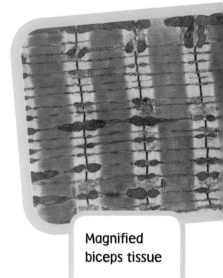

Magnified biceps tissue

Biceps Curl

Do a biceps curl without a weight. Make sure you perform the curl with a smooth movement. With your free hand, feel the way the muscle contracts, or becomes smaller, as you curl in. Do you feel it thicken and tighten?

Then, relax the muscle as you return to the starting position. How does the biceps feel different? You should notice that the muscle elongates. Can you feel it become longer?

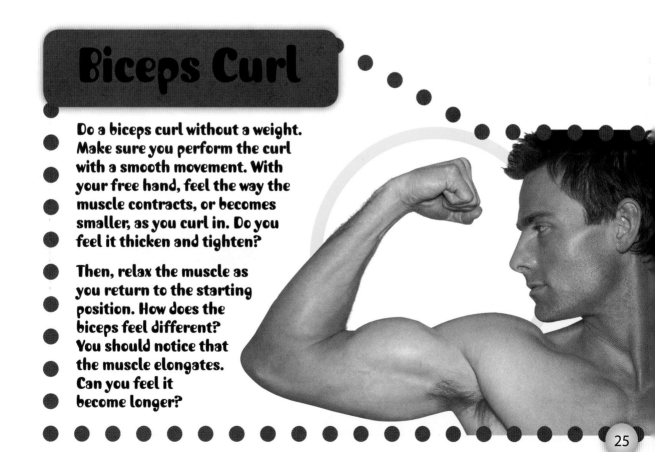

Plant Tissue

You've learned plant cells differ from animal cells. Plant and animal tissues are different, too. There are three major plant tissue types. They are dermal, ground, and vascular tissues.

Dermal tissues protect soft parts of plants. The epidermis is a dermal tissue. It covers the outside of a plant with a waxy, oily coating.

Ground tissues support stems and roots. They function in **photosynthesis** and store food in leaves, stems, and roots.

Vascular tissues are transportation systems. They include **xylem** and **phloem**. Xylem carries water and dissolved minerals up from the roots. It moves them through the stem and leaves. Phloem moves food made in photosynthesis. It carries sugar through the whole plant, all the way down to the roots. This movement of water, minerals, and sugar is called **translocation**.

Phloem moves the food made in photosynthesis. This process is behind the green color.

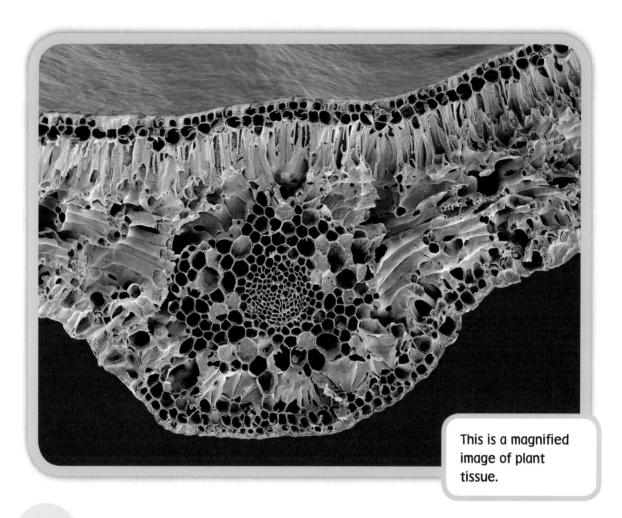

This is a magnified image of plant tissue.

Review

What are the four kinds of human tissue, and what do they do? Connective tissues hold up and connect parts of the body. Epithelial tissues form layers of protection. Muscle tissues contract and relax. Nerve tissues carry messages.

What are the three types of plant tissues? Dermal tissue, ground tissue, and vascular tissue.

What does xylem do? It moves dissolved minerals up from the roots. **How about phloem?** It moves sugar throughout the whole plant and into the roots.

27

Organs

An organ is a complex unit. It's made up of two or more different tissue types. These tissues team together to tackle the same job. Organs are the third level of the hierarchy.

Cells → Tissues → Organs → Organ Systems

Your body is made up of organs. The brain, heart, and lungs are organs. So are the liver, kidneys, and spleen. What's the largest organ of your body? The skin.

The Skin You're In

A living, breathing organ, skin is your fierce protector. In pelting sleet or broiling sunshine, it's the only organ exposed to the environment. What are skin's functions? Tough, flexible, and waterproof, it's a suit of armor. It shields everything inside your body. Skin wrestles with heat and cold.

Our skin protects our bodies.

As an adult, you'll have around 1.9 square meters (20 square feet) of skin. That's the size of a padded backdrop in baseball! Adult skin weighs about 6 pounds.

Made of Different Tissues

Skin contains different tissues. These are hair, sweat glands, fat, muscle, and nerve. **Skin is also made up of three layers**. The outside layer is the **epidermis**. The epidermis is made of **epithelial tissue**.

The **dermis**, a **connective tissue**, is below the epidermis. The dermis holds **nerve tissue**, which allows you to feel. It contains **muscle tissue**, too. That allows movement.

Beneath the dermis is the **subcutaneous layer**. Mostly connective tissue, it holds fat to keep the body warm. It's a protective pillow against injury.

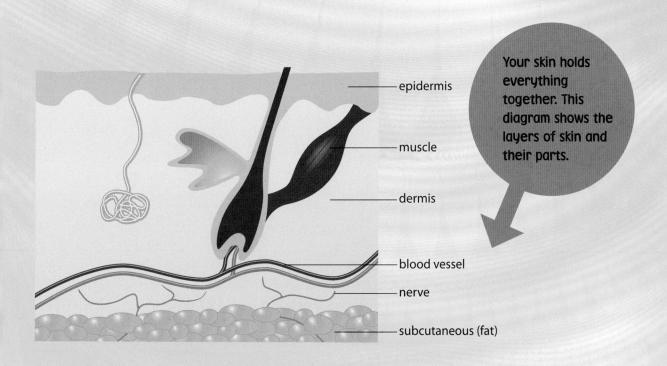

epidermis

muscle

dermis

blood vessel

nerve

subcutaneous (fat)

Your skin holds everything together. This diagram shows the layers of skin and their parts.

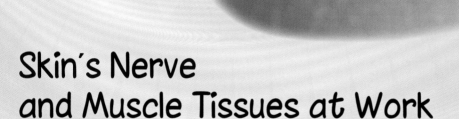

Goose bumps are a response to cold and fear.

Skin's Nerve and Muscle Tissues at Work

How does your body respond when you feel chilly or scared? Little bumps, called goose bumps, rise on your skin. Why does this response take place? First, nerves receive a message that something—maybe a frigid blast of wind—has changed in your environment. It spreads the word to muscle tissues. They contract and tug hair follicles. This causes hairs to stand on end. At the same time, these hairs heat you up. They hold warm air close to your skin.

A similar response takes place in animals that have fur. When they see an enemy, their hairs elevate. It makes them look bigger to their predators.

Plant Organs

Once again, plants are different. Plants are made of two major organs. These are shoots and roots.

The shoots include everything above ground. Stems hold leaves high, toward the sun. That way leaves can snatch as much of the sun's energy as possible. Stems also hold buds, fruit, and flowers. Have you chomped asparagus or bamboo shoots? Both are stems. Leaves are where photosynthesis takes place. Spinach, arugalla, and kale are tasty leaves.

The roots include everything below ground. Roots are in charge of holding the plant in the ground. They might look skinny and spindly, but these gnarly bundles are quite strong. They keep the plant anchored as it grows. When you crunch a carrot or munch a radish, you're eating a root.

These are the main parts of a plant.

leaves

stem

roots

The Brain: Your Body's Control Tower

The brain is your body's control tower, whether you're wide awake or dreaming. Right now, probably without realizing it, you're breathing. Your eyes blink. Your heart is pumping, and your blood is flowing. Maybe your stomach's rumbling, too. The brain is the "brains" of it all.

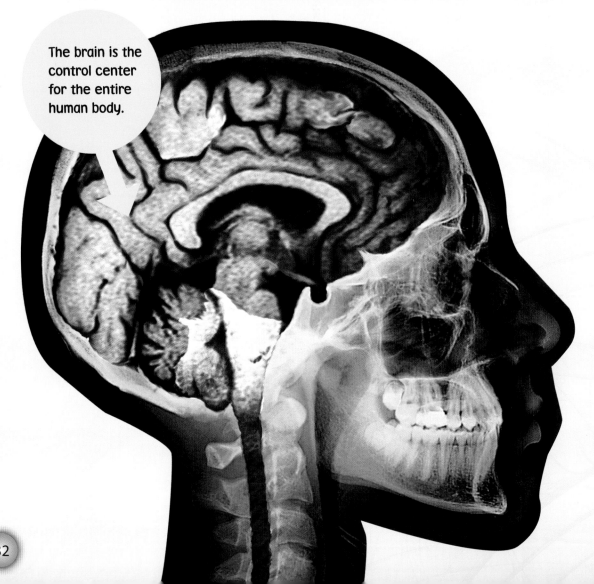

The brain is the control center for the entire human body.

The brain houses your mind. It allows you to think and move. It controls the senses, so you can see, hear, feel, smell, and taste. That's quite a feat for one organ.

ACTIVITY

Stretch your brainpower! Challenge yourself to try something new.

Choose an activity you don't usually do. Compose a song, or choreograph a dance. Create a work of art, do a math equation, or finish a sudoku puzzle.

The brain is in charge of the whole body. But it does not do such a huge job on its own. We'll learn more about the systems of the body in the next chapters. First, let's review organs.

Review

What are organs made of? They are made of two or more different tissue types that work together at the same job.

What are some examples of human body organs? The heart, brain, and lungs are organs. **What's the body's largest organ?** It's the skin.

Plant organs are different. What are the two kinds? They are shoots and roots. **What are some edible plant organs?** Spinach, carrots, and bamboo shoots are edible organs.

Organ Systems

Systems are made up of two or more different organs. These organs work together to tackle the same jobs. Organ systems are the fourth level of the **hierarchy**. The human body is comprised of organ systems.

Cells → Tissues → Organs → Organ Systems

You've learned **cells** form tissues, and tissues form organs. Through further teamwork in your body, organs work together to carry out important functions that keep you alive. These teams are called organ systems.

The Nervous System

Nerves work with the brain and spinal cord to carry messages. Together, they form the nervous system. The nervous system controls reflexes, senses, and movement. When you laugh at a joke, send a text message, or savor a cheesy pizza, your nervous system's at work. It also controls body processes such as digestion. That moves the pizza through your body.

Experience the nervous system in action as you try this. Make a funny face and cross your legs. Jiggle the top leg. Raise and lower your foot.

Your nervous system just directed your movements. It carried electrical signals like instant messages from your brain. They traveled into your spinal cord. From there, motor **neurons** controlled your actions.

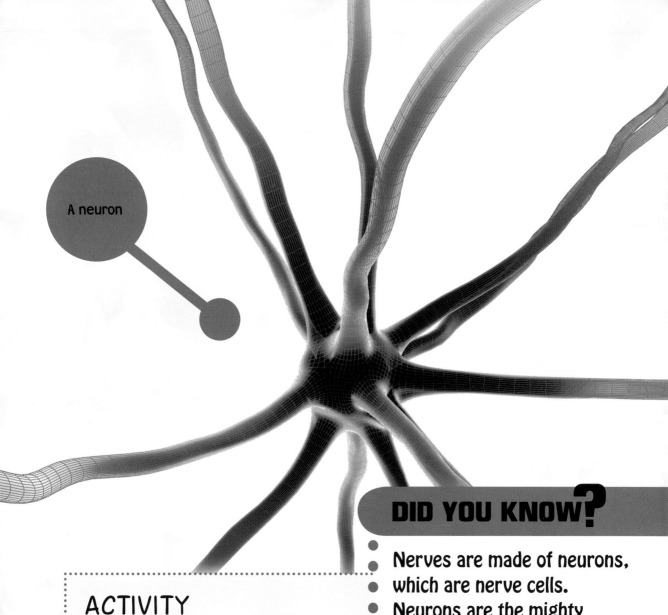

A neuron

Nerves are made of neurons, which are nerve cells. Neurons are the mighty messengers of the nervous system. These electrical bundles look like stretched-out stars. There are 100 billion neurons in your brain. Yep, 100,000,000,000!

ACTIVITY

Check a Friend's Reflexes

Dim the lights in the room. Look into your friend's eyes. Study the pupils and draw a picture of what you see.

Then turn the lights on and repeat. How has the pupil changed? (You should notice that it has shrunk.)

The Respiratory System

Take a deep breath. Inhale through your nose. Now, exhale from your mouth. As you do, gently rest your hands on the sides of your rib cage. How do they change as you breathe in and out? Muscles in your chest and abdomen move so you can breathe.

When you breathe, you bring oxygen into your body. Every cell, every building block of life in your body, needs oxygen. Without it, cells wouldn't survive. And neither would you!

The respiratory system is complicated. Its function is to exchange gases. It takes in the gas oxygen and releases the gas carbon dioxide. The system is made up of the nose, trachea, and lungs.

When you breathe in through the nose, nasal passages work as filters. Hairy cilia and gummy mucous sift away dirt and grit. Nasal passages also warm up and humidify chilly air. Then, they pass air to the back of the throat. Air flows into the trachea (windpipe). From there, the trachea carries air toward the lungs.

DID YOU KNOW?

It takes about 2 liters (4.2 pints) of air to fill a basketball. The average person's lungs hold 3–5 liters (6.3–10.6 pints).

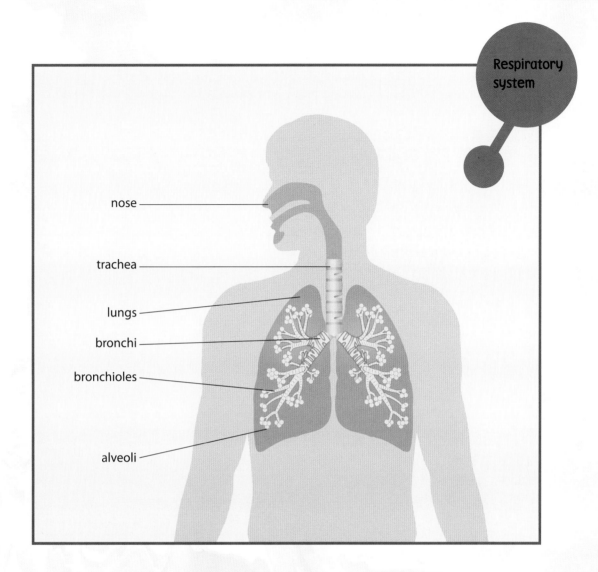

nose

trachea

lungs

bronchi

bronchioles

alveoli

As you see in the diagram, the trachea branches into two tubes. These tubes are *bronchi*. *Bronchi* are the main passages that connect to lungs. Inside the lungs are smaller and smaller tubes. These are *bronchioles*. At the tips of teeny *bronchioles* are air sacs called *alveoli*. *Alveoli* exchange carbon dioxide for oxygen. They move carbon dioxide out of, and oxygen into, your blood.

The Circulatory System

The circulatory system is also known as the cardiovascular system. One of the most important body systems, it's formed of the heart, blood vessels, and blood. The system's function is to move blood, oxygen, and nutrients to all the body parts. It also helps clear out wastes.

Clench your fist. That's around the size of your heart, one of the strongest muscles in your body. Like other muscles, it contracts and relaxes. The heart pumps blood through chambers and blood vessels. Arteries move blood away from the heart. Veins carry blood back.

For most people between 12 and 60, the heart beats an average of 60–90 times per minute. For athletes, the rate is usually 40–60. Right now, as you read, you're experiencing a resting heart rate. What happens when you pump up your activity? Your heart rate increases.

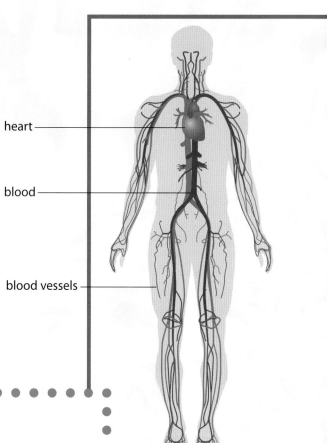

heart

blood

blood vessels

Heart Rate

Find your pulse using two fingers. Place them on your wrist or at the side of your neck. Don't press too hard.

Take your resting heart rate for six seconds. Write down the number of beats you counted.

Now, calculate the number of beats per minute. How? Multiply the number by 10. Write down your new number.

Finally, run in place for one minute and repeat. How do the results differ?

System	Function	Main Parts	Example of the System at Work
Nervous	To control movement, reflexes	Brain, spinal cord, nerves	Pain felt when toe gets stubbed
Respiratory	To take in oxygen and release carbon dioxide	Nose, trachea, lungs, bronchi, alveoli	Deep breathing when running
Circulatory	To move oxygen and nutrients through the body	Heart, blood, blood vessels	Higher heart rate when playing hockey
Digestive	To break down food, receive nutrients from it, and turn it into waste	Mouth, saliva, esophagus, stomach, intestines, pancreas, liver, gall bladder, rectum	Gurgling stomach after eating
Immune	To prevent infection and keep the body healthy	Skin, bone marrow, adenoids, tonsils, lymph nodes, blood vessels, lymphatic vessels	Healing wound on kneecap

Review

Two or more organs work together to form **organ systems**. The human body is made up of important systems. This chart reviews information you've learned. It adds information about the digestive and immune systems, too. Hey, why not? We have plenty of important systems in our bodies!

Out-of-Control Cells

When **cells** grow abnormally, they cause cancer. Cancer cells don't stop growing. Instead, they invade healthy tissues and organs.

You've learned about the extraordinary teamwork of cells, tissues, organs, and organ systems. When cells go bad, it can affect the whole **hierarchy**.

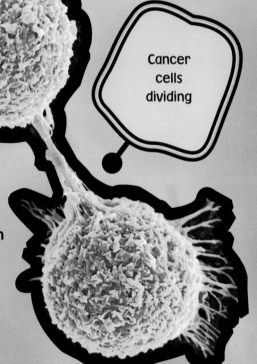

Cancer cells dividing

A Domino Effect of Destruction

When a normal cell divides, it splits. One cell becomes two. Since cells know their job descriptions, they know when to stop dividing.

Cancer cells are different. Cancer is a disease caused when normal cells change and rapidly grow. Cancer cells reproduce without stopping. One cell splits into two. Then two become four, and so on.

Cancer cells cause a domino effect of destruction. Out-of-control cells cluster. They form a lump, or tumor. The tumor spreads to neighboring tissues. When the tumor swarms healthy tissues and organs, it destroys them. As a result, a person grows extremely ill.

A Strange Change

Sophia noticed a strange change in the mole on her shoulder. Usually brown, the mole had turned black. Red blotches dotted it. Usually smooth, the mole now felt crusty. Its shape was irregular. Sophia visited the doctor. She received the frightening diagnosis—melanoma. This is the deadliest form of skin cancer. A doctor would need to treat the disease with surgery.

Attacking the Invader

Through surgery, Sophia's doctor removed as many cancer cells as possible. The doctor also removed surrounding healthy tissues and cells. This was an extra precaution to make certain all of the cancer was cleared out.

Other methods of treating cancer include radiation and chemotherapy, called "chemo." In radiation treatment, doctors use high-energy waves to wipe out cancer cells and shrink tumors.

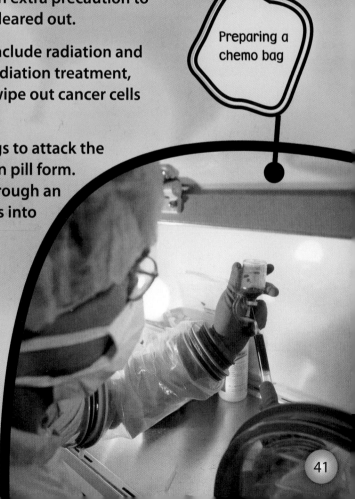

Preparing a chemo bag

With chemo, a patient receives drugs to attack the disease. Sometimes medicines are in pill form. Often, the patient receives them through an IV placed into a vein. Medicine flows into the blood. It travels through the body to wipe out cancer cells.

Cancer touches many lives. You might know someone who has bravely battled the disease or even died from it. Yet, there is hopeful news. Thanks to early detection and medical advances, survival rates have increased.

Review and Quiz

You've learned about the cell, the basic unit of life. You know it's part of a system of organization, the hierarchy of cells, tissues, organs, and systems. Now, take this quiz to check up on what you've learned!

Fill in the Blank

1. Cells are called life's _____.

2. Every living thing is made of _____.

3. The part of the brain that monitors temperature is the _____.

4. Cells combine oxygen and food to get _____.

5. _____ first discovered plant cells and used the word *cells*.

Multiple Choice

1. The little parts inside of cells are called_____.

   a. organs

   b. organelles

   c. animalcules

   d. blobs

2. Antoni van Leeuwenhoek discovered_____.

   a. plant cells

   b. bacteria

   c. tartar

   d. sickle cell anemia

3. Plant and animal cells cannot survive without a_____.

   a. tissue

   b. membrane

   c. nucleus

   d. system

4. What is one feature that makes a plant cell different from an animal cell?

    a. A plant cell is alive.

    b. A plant cell doesn't have a nucleus.

    c. A plant cell has chloroplasts.

    d. A plant cell can't make its own food.

5. Blood is a _____ tissue.

    a. muscle

    b. nerve

    c. connective

    d. epithelial

Short Answer

1. Use your experiences in completing the biceps curl to describe how muscle tissues contract and relax.

2. Why are plant vascular tissues considered transportation systems?

Illustrations

1. Choose one of the human body systems. Make a drawing to illustrate how it works.

2. Make a drawing to illustrate how cancer cells increase.

Answer Key:

Fill in the Blank

1. building blocks
2. cells
3. hypothalamus
4. energy
5. Robert Hooke

Multiple Choice

1. b, 2. b, 3. c, 4. c, 5. c

Short Answer

1. Possible response: When I did the biceps curl, my muscle tightened and felt bunched up and firm. When I let my arm relax, the biceps seemed to flatten out and get softer

2. Possible response: Vascular tissues contain xylem and phloem, which move water, sugar, and minerals through a plant.

Illustrations

Drawings will vary.

Organs and Tissues and Cells — Oh My!

Miles and Miles

Your skin contains 72,400 kilometers (45,000 miles) of nerves. That's the distance between Miami, Florida, and Bimini in the Bahamas.

How many miles of blood vessels does a person have? A whopping 96,500 kilometers (60,000 miles)! Enough to loop Earth well over two times.

The Skinny on Skin

Inside one square inch of your skin are 6.1 meters (20 feet) of blood vessels. They could stretch as high as a two-story building.

Every 28 days or so, you shed old skin cells and grow new ones. You'll sprout 1,000 new skins during your life!

Have a Heart

- Your heart beats all day, every day, all through your life. In a year, it beats around 30 million times.

- Let's say your heart beats 70 times per minute. By the time you're 70, it will beat about 2.5 billion times.

- The heart feels firm, yet it gives. If you squeezed it, it would feel like an orange.

- Why is your left lung smaller than the right? So there's room for the heart!

Be a Braniac

- The brain is the consistency of overcooked, rubbery cauliflower!

- The brain is nearly 85 percent water. No wonder it's jiggly!

- Neanderthals (prehistoric, manlike creatures) had larger brains than people have today.

Muscle Bound

There are more than 600 muscles in the human body. In the face alone, there are 60. Smiling uses 17 muscles. Frowning takes 43!

The largest muscle in the body is the gluteus maximus, the buttock. Why are glutes big? They hold the torso in place. These mighty muscles also help legs swing toward the, um, rear to climb, run, and walk.

Glossary

Bacteria Single-celled microorganisms

Cancer Disease caused when cells grow out of control and attack healthy tissues and organs

Cell Basic, microscopic part of a living thing

Chlorophyll Green chemical in plants that gives them their color

Chloroplast Organelle of a plant in which photosynthesis takes place

Chromosome Rod-shaped part of a cell that holds genes; found inside the nucleus

Collagen Fibrous protein found in connective tissue, bone, and cartilage

Connective tissue Animal tissue that supports and connects the body

Dermal tissue Plant tissue that protects soft plant parts

Epithelial tissue Animal tissue that protects and lines the body

Fibroblast Large, flat cells that make collagen

Gene Part that determines traits and is passed from parents to offspring

Ground tissue Plant tissue that supports stems and roots

Hierarchy A way of organizing something or breaking it into levels

Hypothalamus The part of the brain that controls temperature

Muscle tissue Specialized animal tissue that contracts and relaxes

Nerve tissue Animal tissue that transmits electrical signals

Neuron Nerve cell that makes up nervous tissue

Nucleus Largest and central part of a cell; the cell's "brain"

Organelle Little part that, along with other organelles, makes up a cell and has its own function

Phloem Plant tissue that moves sugar manufactured in photosynthesis throughout a plant

Photosynthesis Process by which green plants use energy from the sun to make their own food

Platelet Piece of a cell in the blood that helps blood clot, or thicken

Protozoa Single-celled animal organisms

Respiration Process by which cells obtain energy through combining food and oxygen

Translocation Movement of water, minerals, and sugar from one part of a plant to another

Vascular tissue Plant tissue that transports materials throughout the plant

Xylem Plant tissue that carries minerals and water from plant roots

Further Information

Books to read

Farndon, John. *Science Experiments: The Human Body*. Tarrytown, NY: Marshall Cavendish, 2002.

Katz, Nevin. *Dr. Birdley Teaches Science: Introducing Cells*. Nashville, TN: Incentive Publications, 2007.

Snedden, Robert. *The World of the Cell*. Chicago: Heinemann, 2008.

Spilsbury, Louise, and Richard Spilsbury. *Super-Flea and Other Animal Champions: Cells, Tissues, and Organs*. Chicago: Raintree, 2006.

Stansfield, William, Raul J. Cano, and Jaime S. Colome. *Schaum's Easy Outlines: Molecular and Cell Biology*. New York: MacGraw-Hill, 2003.

Stille, Darlene R. *Cells*. Strongsville, OH: Gareth Stevens, 2008.

Trefil, James, Rita Ann Calvo, and Kenneth Cutler. *Cells and Heredity*. Evanston, IL: McDougal Littell, 2004.

Websites

http://americanhistory.si.edu/anatomy/index.html
Take a peek inside the human body at this fascinating site!

http://www.youtube.com/watch?v=fQNrW8O9I10
Follow the amazing circuit of a red blood cell through the human body in this video.

http://faculty.washington.edu/chudler/chmemory.html
Stretch your brainpower with memory games and more at this website.

http://www.sciencenews.org/view/interest/id/3/topic/Science_News_For_Kids
Read great science articles and test your knowledge at this fact-filled site.

http://sciencespot.net/Pages/kidzone.html
This site provides links to all types of science (earth, life, and physical). You can find out more about cells, tissues, and organs!

Index